A WORKMAN FOR
GOD

ALBERTA BETTY ROVETO

ISBN 978-1-0980-4363-6 (paperback)
ISBN 978-1-0980-4364-3 (digital)

Christian Faith Publishing, Inc.
832 Park Avenue
Meadville, PA 16335
www.christianfaithpublishing.com

Printed in the United States of America

Poems for My Heavenly Father

I offer you these poems, Father,
They are written from my heart.
I offer you these poems in which
You did take part.

You have graced me with your love, Father,
Which give them harmony.
The inspiration from your word,
Has a message for all who seek.

I offer you these poems, Father,
I am grateful for your spiritual seed,
You uphold me with your righteous arm,
Thy strength is mine indeed.

I offer so little, heavenly Father,
For the gifts you've given me.
There is my faith, and my poems,
Which reveal my love for Thee.

Psalms 95:2

A Workman for God

As workmen for God, we travel light,
Stewarding His Word the best we can,
We let people know God has a plan,
It is to save the world from the grip of Satan.

Most people choose not to believe,
God's Word is His gift to all who will cleave.
It is not laden with hardship, or burden you see,
The Word is the key to living happily.

God gave us His son the Lord Jesus Christ,
To lean on in times of fear or strife,

Satan's deceptions are real but we can win!
The Word is the answer its power is so neat,
It knocks Satan down each time in defeat,
And brings us up to God's royal seat.

Now when worry and doubt put a strain on your day,
Pick up God's Word without delay.
Take a stand, endure, and make Satan pay,
Remember God's gift His Word, His Way.

2 Timothy 2:15

For we are God's HANDIWORK, CREATED IN CHRIST JESUS TO DO GOOD WORKS, WHICH GOD PREPARED IN ADVANCE FOR US TO DO.

EPHESIANS 2:10

Believing and Achieving

I'm believing and achieving in my walk
With God each day my strength is in His hands
God's Word I will obey.

I am walking and I am talking to all who may
Take heed, God is my sufficiency He supplies
My every need.

I am capable and worthy; my fears I've left behind.
Knowing I have Christ in me has renewed and
Strengthened my mind.

My future is much brighter and I'm forging straight
Ahead I'm believing and achieving in my walk
With God, my Stead!

Philippians 3:13–14

For I know the plans I have for you," declares the Lord , "plans to prosper you and not to harm you, plans to give you hope and a future.

Jeremiah 29:11

Champions for the Lord Jesus Christ

We are champions for the Lord,
We are contending for Christ!
He has sacrificed his life that we might win,
There is no condemnation, a new life we begin.

We are champions for the Lord,
He is the 'Bread of Life'
With God's word as our shield,
Whatever the challenge we do not yield.

We are champions for the Lord,
We are the children of light.
Believing God's Word elevates us to new heights,
Renewed in the spirit and ready to fight.

We are champions for the Lord,
We are contending for Christ!

1 Timothy 6:12

Contentment

How many of us can say we are content,
Is it not a fact we all have a need to vent?

What does it take to feel so free?
Does it help to know it's God in Christ in thee?

Are we content when we say,
I walked with the Lord today?

God's creation, how majestic the event,
Does it make our heart peaceful and content?

Let us look up, and be thankful, for morning and eve.
Lift our voices in song; and put our hearts at ease.

At day's end let us pray to God, as we should,
God will see, and say, it is very good!

Hebrews 13:5

Established, Rooted, and Grounded

We are established, rooted, and grounded,
God's Word through us is expounded.
God gave us the right to stand bold in His sight,
We make known the Lord, Jesus Christ.

In God's Word we are established,
We study and follow its keys,
We know the Father loves us,
And we do all we can to please.

The gift is a spiritual treasure,
Our wealth is in the Lord,
Our lives reveal God's pleasure,
Sharing His truth we are in one accord.

We search the scriptures daily,
And consume every word,
We then herald forth the knowledge,
For it is hungering to be heard.

In God's Word we are rooted,
Our believing remains unwavered,
With the Father we are one,
We are sanctified and righteous through His son.

In ministering we continue to grow,
It is His love God wants us to know,
One heart, one mind, one body,
Through us the 'Good News' will be told.

Our efforts are never unnoticed,
And our fruit is always abounding,
We have incorruptible seed,
And the power we have is astounding!

In God's Word we are grounded,
We have put off our old man nature,
To our past there is no returning,
We have set those bridges burning.

Our believing is strong and secure,
We stand on a firm foundation,
We are precious in God's sight,
We have no condemnation!

Our quest is to stand against adversity,
Our immovable force is the Lord, Jesus Christ.
Through him we will conquer, and live the
More abundant life.

It is the will of our heavenly Father above,
That His children be,
Established, rooted, and grounded in love.

Ephesians 3:17

I set My
rainbow in the
clouds, and it
shall be a sign
of a covenant
between Me
and the earth.
Genesis 9:13

God Sees the Heart

Where will I be when I hear God's trumpet, His call,
I may be at a park, or maybe at a shopping mall?
Winter, Spring, Summer, or Fall,
The season will not matter at all.

What will I wear when I am called to the sky?
Oh I know fashion will not matter up on high,
I will be changed in the blink of an eye.

I know I'll look my very best,
For my spirit will ascend to thee,
For it is the heart God sees, and not the dress.

1 Samuel 16:7

God's Garden, God's Word

Come to My garden array with vivid hue,
Come to the garden I created for you.

I have blessed it with promises, wisdom and such,
I have blessed it for you, come see and touch.

It is fragrant beyond all your wildest dreams,
Rainbows adorn every tingling stream.

Come to My garden it is peaceful and bright,
My son is the source of its exuberant light.

Come to My garden, and make it your own,
Come to My garden, and make it your home.

Isaiah 58:11

Laborer for the Harvest

Heavenly Father, You have chosen me to be a laborer,
And you shall teach me Thy Truths.
Heavenly Father, You have chosen me to be a laborer,
And Your request I shall not refuse.
Heavenly Father, I never labored for a harvest.
I never tended a great field, but I shall hold forth my basket,
And my heart to You I'll yield.

Luke 10:2

1 Corinthians 3:9

My Tattered Holy Bible

My Holy Bible tattered and worn,
The tassel still hangs from its pages frayed and torn.
The years that were spent in its truth and wisdom,
The knowledge obtained about God and His kingdom.

My Holy Bible tattered and worn,
We celebrated life, but there are those we did mourn.
I lift its frail cover and listed inside,
Generations of family it helped mold and guide.

The Bible has truths of courage, faithful deeds, and Christ's life,
It has psalms of comfort, of great joy, and delight.
It lays on my night stand never far from sight,
At times I would hold it for strength through the night.

My Holy Bible tattered and worn,
The tassel still hangs from its pages frayed and torn,
Although it is frail the message lives and reigns,
It is the light and the key to our heavenly Father's domain.

Matthew 24:35

Our Sonship Rights

Our faith in Jesus Christ has deemed us blessed,
Chosen of Almighty God, Righteous children in His household.

$$2 \text{ Corinthians } 5:21$$

Redemption is a beautiful thing,
Jesus, our savior, sacrificed His life and paid the ultimate price.

$$\text{Ephesians } 1:7$$

Sanctified by His blood, our fate is sealed
We are seated in the heavenlies, no longer living in fear.

$$1 \text{ Corinthians } 1:2$$

Now we are Justified, and boldly stand before God,
No guilt! No condemnation!

$$1 \text{ Corinthians } 6:11$$

Our heavenly Father trusts us to boldly speak for Him.
We are blessed to have the Ministry of Reconciliation.

$$2 \text{ Corinthians } 5:18$$

Satan Is Real

Satan is real, his motive is to steal,
Every heart from the Lord Jesus Christ,
Beware! God warns! Satan's deceptions look bright,
But he comes like a thief in the night.

Satan will try to destroy if he can, God's gift to His Children.
God's royal plan to save His household from the grip of Satan,
God's Word is the shield; its knowledge opens doors,
Its keys are the weapon we need to contend.

The word teaches Christ, His way, His truth, and His life.
Fear not! Stand strong! Believe God's Word,
Walk upright, stay faithful serving the Lord with delight,
This is God's promise He will guide you through the perils of night.

John 10:10

Step by Step

Step by step, mile by mile I know my God, I am your child.
Day by day, week by week, my walk with you does increase.
Minute by minute, hour by hour, I claim Your Word, my high tower.

Step by step, mile by mile, I know my life may have some trials.
Day by day, week by week, my God's strength is all I seek.
Because of your dear Son's great deed I now have God in Christ in me.
Minute by minute, hour by hour, I speak in tongues, and manifest
God's power.

Psalm 37:23

Teach the World to Sing

Teach the world how to sing,
And make God's Word the music.

Teach the children a new song,
And God's Word will be the lyrics.

Teach the neighbors harmony,
Let God's Word do the fine tuning.

Teach the world another hymn,
In honor of Christ's returning.

A song in the heart, peace it implores,
The heart in a song praising God,
Shall have its rewards.

Psalms 100

Thank You for My Day

Thank you for my day, Lord
Your word has surely blessed me.

"All Thine are mine, and mine are Thine"
"I in them and Thou in me."

I recalled these words thankfully,
And the adversary's hurling darts did flee.

As I praised you at length,
I felt God's love and God's strength.

My day, instead of stressful and weary,
Was won in joyful victory!

As I rest my head on my pillow tonight,
I thank you Lord, for you are the light of life.

John 17:10

The Lord Jesus Christ Says, Seek Me!

Seek my face for I am the image of my Father.

Seek my heart for it is pure love.

Seek my arms for they reach out imploring know me.

Seek my hands for in them are where yours should be.

Seek my legs for they walk in truth.

Seek my feet for they make prints for life

Truly believe, that when you seek me, you seek our heavenly Father,

And in His kingdom you shall have eternal life.

Proverbs 8:17

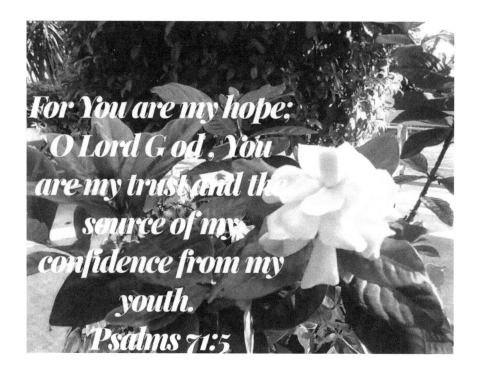

For You are my hope;
O Lord G od , You
are my trust and the
source of my
confidence from my
youth.
Psalms 71:5

The Seasons of Life

Spring arrives, and as the vibrant sun rises
Youth rides its spirited stallion across the
Emerald plane, challenging the thunder
And lightning of season rains.

It's summer a rainbow of pastel dreams
Array the bright blue sky and float upon drifting
Clouds of wishful thinking, and believing promises

Autumn approaches, the auburn leaves rustle under
The steed's hooves, gentle laughter is heard, and
There is the murmur of a crisp rippling brook

Winter enters with a chill. Its golden light drifts
Amid the platinum hills, leisurely life fades into obscure shadow.
The sun sets in a blaze of fire, darkness falls and the season ends.

A Love Letter

God bless you, I say this from my heart,
I love you, these words to you I impart.
You were such joy amid the hectic daily pace,
Never thought we would fall apart and bicker face to face.

I felt so very sad I wept, it hurt so badly.
No matter how I tried I could not mend the hurt inside me.
I'm thankful for the time we've spent
God will mend my broken heart.

Someday perhaps with God's grace I pray,
You will know what I have found.
In God's Word the truth is known,
How Satan does deceive.

Until you let God in your heart, praise Him every day,
Mention Jesus Christ in thanks, whenever you do pray,
Your eyes will never see the devil spirit realm,
That keeps the wall between us up instead of knocking it down?

2 Corinthians 6:14

Galatians 5:7

My Heavenly Father, Abba, Lives Here!

My *LORD*, *Jehovah* is the Living God, His blessings do abound.
It is God, in Christ, in me, I stand on hallowed ground.
By God's grace I was saved, not by any works of mine.
Jesus Christ is the source, salvation for all mankind.
Together we stand, clasping our Father's hand.
There is no doubt, no worry nor fear, and I am very confident,
Abba, lives here!

Romans 8:15

Christ Knocks at the Door of Doubt

Jesus walked this earth a sinless man; He sacrificed Himself at the cross.
This act of selfless courage gave the believer eternal life.
Jesus, our savior, lived and died to save the world.
Yet there are those who refuse to acknowledge He is the Son of God.

Jesus is so gracious and generous He lives today, knocking on every
denying heart, saying,
Let Me erase the cloud of doubt, and manifest God's light.
Come to the Savior Jesus Christ, declare Him as Lord,
Believe and your name shall be etched in the book of life.

Revelations 1:18; 3:5, 20

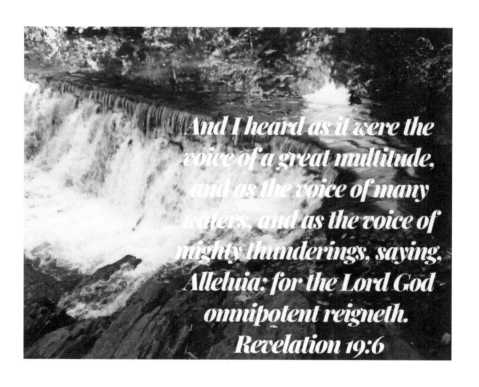

And I heard as it were the voice of a great multitude, and as the voice of many waters, and as the voice of mighty thunderings, saying, Alleluia: for the Lord God omnipotent reigneth. Revelation 19:6

Fellowship with Jesus Christ

Jesus, it's you and I in fellowship,
The thought is so profound.
It's you and I side by side,
We walk on holy ground.

What a twosome! What a pair!
We're so unique it is God we share.
I often wonder where I'd be
If you didn't give your life for me,

Jesus, I'm just so grateful for your love,
And with you, I'll always rise above,
All who doubt, and fail to see,
It's you and I in heavenly places.

Ephesians 2:6

God Can Do the Impossible

Do we believe God is still a miracle God?
Why is there doubt, worry, fear?
Let us claim God's healing for body, mind, and spirit.

Jesus Christ says, "Ask in My name and the Father shall do."
This promise is for me, as well as for you.
Satan is powerless when we claim his defeat.
The snake in the grass is under our feet.

We must stand our ground, patience is the key.
God backs up His Word with power and truth.
Stay firm and positive, continue in this belief.

Believers, do you not discern and understand that
You are God's temple, His permanent place,
And He will rebuke the devourer for our sakes.

Yes God can do the impossible we can claim it and believe,
He will open the windows of heaven, pouring out blessings,
And there shall not be room enough for us to receive.

Matthew 19:26

Malachi 3:10–11

God's Tapestry

God's tapestry for our lives is a special weave of love,
Blessed by our heavenly Father,
God's tapestry is strong, colorful, and joyful in promise.

God's tapestry is intricately woven throughout God's Word.
And helps us to endure the attacks of the adversary,
God's tapestry gives us victory.

God's tapestry is rare, never to be duplicated,
Yet available for all to marvel and touch.

God's tapestry for our lives is the Lord, Jesus Christ.
He suffered, died, and has risen.
God's tapestry lives today!
And He is the only covering we'll ever need.

Matthew 8:27

HE WILL COVER YOU WITH HIS
FEATHERS, AND UNDER HIS WINGS YOU
WILL FIND REFUGE, HIS FAITHFULNESS
will be your shield and rampart.

PSALM 91:4

I Go To Prepare A Place For You

Jesus said, In My father's house are many mansions.
If it was not so I would have told you.

John 14:2

I go to the Father and wait for you
I go to prepare a place.
A place where sunshine glows from within
Where rainbows have no end,

A place of peaceful serenity
Worship without profanity.
I go to the Father and wait for you
I go to prepare a place
A place of pure unselfish love,
Where your spirit soars like an eagle
A place where freedom is not challenged
Where hymns of praise are not silenced
I go to the Father and wait for you
I go to prepare a place.
Where death and suffering are no more.
A place where God our Father invites you to stay
Where He alone created the way
I go to the Father and wait for you
I go to prepare a place
A place where I, Jesus, am the fountain of living waters
A place where we shall live together as holy sons and daughters

And now these three remain: faith, hope and love. But the greatest of these is love. 1 Corinthians 13:13

Never Deny the Lord Jesus Christ

Never deny the Lord Jesus Christ,
He is our shield, our buckler,
Our strength, and comfort in times of strife.

Never deny the Lord Jesus Christ,
It was for us He laid down His life,
That He might be our guiding light.

Never deny the Lord Jesus Christ,
It was for love He made the ultimate sacrifice.
He is watching, and waiting, guiding our way.
For our Lord Jesus Christ, lives today!

Ephesians 1:20

Who Is the Born Again Believer?

I am child of the living God, a force of nature. The Lord, Jesus says my believing can move mountains. (Luke 20:36)

The born again believer, who am I?

I am the light of the world, and the enemy of darkness, I am a city on a hill, an illumination of God's love. (John 12:36; Ephesians 5:8)

The born again believer, who am I?

I am a witness, a testimony of salvation and spiritual change. I was saved by Christ my savior His sacrifice opened the door of God's amazing grace. (Ephesians 2:5)

The born again believer, who am I?

I am the apple of my heavenly Father's eye. He has given me His Holy Spirit, and I am protected by His supernatural hedge. (Psalm 17:8)

The born again believer, who am I?

I am a chosen vessel. I have Christ in me the hope of glory. I share an inheritance of everlasting life with the Lord Jesus Christ.

(Ephesians 1:4; Colossians 1:27; Hebrews 9:15)

I am a born again believer!

Prayer, Make It Perfect!

God's gift to you, His Holy Spirit,
Thank Him well, and celebrate!
Speak in tongues, make it perfect.

When you speak, and share your heart,
You will know The Father is taking part,
Speak in tongues make it perfect.

Do you have a need today? Believe!
God's power when you pray,
Speak in tongues make it perfect.

As we live His Word we abound in grace,
The gift is ours with The Father's embrace,
Thank Him well speak in tongues,

Make it perfect!

1 Corinthians 14:2

Singing in Harmony for the Lord

Singing in harmony we are heralding for Christ,
Singing in harmony makes witnessing twice as nice.
Singing in harmony, it's Christ's love within us flaming,
Sing along; sing along, it's our joy we are proclaiming.

Sing along; sing along, we are charging forth to give good news,
Sing along; sing along, we are giving the word that is hungering to
    be heard.

Singing in harmony we are spreading God's Word throughout the nation,
Singing in harmony we are professing God's love with elation,
Sing along, sing along, and let's confess with adulation,
It's God, in Christ, in you, this is our strong foundation.

Ephesians 5:19

KEEP ME AS THE
APPLE OF YOUR EYE;
HIDE ME IN THE
SHADOW OF YOUR WINGS

PSALMS 17:8

The Return

One day we'll sit together, Lord, alongside our Father's throne.

I know because you told me so, I read it in God's Word.

You'll return again and gather all who love you here on earth.

I know because it was promised

When we receive the spiritual new birth.

Until then I'll wait dear Jesus for the trumpet of God to sound,

Announcing Your timely return.

Our hope of everlasting life and eternity with God.

1 Corinthians 15:52

A Pledge and a Promise

God's Word is God's pledge and His promise,

It is the testament of knowledge for life.

It is the pledge of support, and the promise of strength,

The same which was given to the Lord Jesus Christ.

God's Word is God's pledge and His promise,

The Word is God's Will

It is the pledge of love, and the promise of glory,

It is the powerful javelin in the spiritual fight.

God's Word is God's pledge and His promise,

For those who believe it is the Way of Life

It is the pledge of truth, and the promise of hope,

It is the treasure of our Father's delight.

2 Peter 1:3–4

Understanding God's Word

Is

'The Spice of Life'

I am faithful, steadfast, and encouraged when challenges arise,
I don't worry about tomorrow, and I've left the past behind.

I use godly wisdom in my walk when dealing with mankind,
If I stay the course of light there's no mountain I can't climb.

I keep myself in balance God's knowledge, His word opens doors,
It's the road to spiritual understanding, a beacon through the night.

I am confident in knowing I have the 'Spice of Life.'

Ephesians 1:18

AS WATER REFLECTS
THE FACE, SO ONE'S
LIFE REFLECTS
the heart.
PROVERBS 27:19

Be Strong in the Lord

Be strong in the Lord, praise Him every day!
Believe His word will sustain thee,
God's Way is the true way.

Be strong in the Lord,
As children of the most High God, we walk as light,
We are endowed with grace and His awesome might.

Be strong in the Lord be faithful!
Developing a bold and confident walk of power,
For great is our God's presence hour by hour.

Be strong in the Lord, no doubt, no worry, no fear!
This is the path of victory, knowing the Father is near,
We daily endeavor to defeat the enemy.

Ephesians 6:10

Contend against Adversity

Contend against adversity,
Run the course put up a fight.
Contend against adversity,
Show God's power and His might.

Contend against adversity,
Put on God's love don't be shy.
Be not ignorant and know God's Word,
Stay on guard, be strong in the Lord.

You can win against adversity,
You can win if you don't faint.
You can win against adversity,
You're God's child, you're a saint.

Christ contended in the arena,
He paid the price for all.
He showed the devil, who is boss,
He answered the Father's call.

Contend against adversity, be a spiritual athlete
For God hath promised in His Word,
Satan shall go down in flames,
And ye shall triumph over his defeat.

Ephesians 6:12

Cast Your Care upon Jesus

Cast your care upon Jesus,
Cast your care upon Him.
Cast your care upon the Lord,
He has freed us from sin.

Let Him carry your burden,
Let Him lighten the load.
Cast your care upon the Lord,
He shall pave every road.

Trust Him to lift the weight off your shoulders,
Trust Him and He will enrich you with boldness.

Cast your care upon Jesus,
It's what He wants you to do.
Cast your care upon the Lord,
He desires to love you.

He shall do His utmost when we do our best,
He shall release us from fear, worry, and stress.

Cast your care upon Jesus,
Lean on His chest.
Cast your care upon the Lord,
In His arms you shall find rest.

1 Peter 5:7

Get Carried Away

Take a journey through ancient time,
And learn lessons for future endeavor.
God's Word is your pathway for the abundant life,
Explore and find its treasures.
Great are the lessons and resources God gives.
His truths will guide you through life, Forever.

Isaiah 35:8

God Direct My Steps
A Prayer

God, direct my steps,
Keep me alert and at my best,
Always walking with you in love,

God, direct my speech,
Let each word I utter be filled with wisdom,
I want always to speak the truth in love.

God, I want always to listen to your voice within me,
To lift each thought to you with joyful
Believing, perfection, and love.

God, direct my spirit which is your gift.
I want always to manifest at my full potential.
I thank you for your everlasting grace, mercy, and love. Amen.

Proverbs 16:9

God's Church

God's church is not a building built with stucco, wood, or stone,
It is anywhere my children gather believing in God's word,
Living life abundantly, making Jesus Christ their own.

It could be on the desert or in a mountain cave,
It is anywhere my children praise the Lord making a joyful sound,
This is where God is, and where His grace abounds.

God's church is not a building built with stucco, wood, or stone,
It is anywhere two or three are gathered worshiping in prayer,
They know God their Father, hears them, and are confident He is there.

Zephaniah 3:17

Matthew 18:20

Let Go and Let God

I am the Great Redeemer, I understand your pain.
It was for you I gave my Son, that He should bear it all.
My child let go, and cease from all your efforts,
Let Me control the reigns.

I am your Mighty Fortress, the Light to guide your way,
I've given you My Spirit it is great strength in time of pain.
My child, let go and know that I am God! I uphold you
With My loving arms and I walk with you each day.

Inspiration—Psalm 46

In God's Favor

I know it's not through my own labor God gives me His divine favor.
It is faith in my Lord Jesus Christ that grace may abound in my life.
God's grace is all that I need, and like His son I am favored indeed.

The joy that I might boast, my life is content because of my heavenly
host.
It is Christ Jesus who set me apart, and with His love I will live and
achieve.
And God's grace His divine favor is truly my sufficiency as long as I
believe.

Romans 15:13

My God Reigns

My God, You are all knowing and wise.
In Your faithful heart there is no compromise.

When You say, God's will be done.
It means be still and know the battle has already been won.

What price was paid, what ultimate cost?
You gave Your son to die on a cross.

The gain is ours, with His precious blood,
He bought atonement for all who are lost.

My God, Your love sustains all who believe,
There is hope, and a future, a promise you gave.

A life in Christ Jesus could be achieved,
And a seat by God's throne is victory indeed.

2 Timothy 2:11–12

Revelation 3:21

Reaching for the Father's Hand

Whenever I reach, Father, you take my hand,
I trust you as a child and you help me to understand.

Your shadow does not hide me from sight,
You guide me from behind and made me the light.

As I continue to grow I'm nurtured with
Thy word and Thy love,
I am so proud to say, "My Father is God above."
With each day I grow more confident in the word you teach,
I trust you, Father, to take my hand, whenever I reach.

Psalm 71:5

The voice of the Lord is upon the waters: The God of glory thunders; The Lord is over many waters. Psalms 29:3

Our Identity in Christ

Our identity in Christ is a relationship with Him.
It is the gateway of freedom, the door of light and love.
We have Christ's peace, God's Spirit, and righteous blessing from
    above.

Our identity in Christ is our inheritance, and the promise of eternal
    favor begins.
God gave His only begotten and beloved Son to sacrifice His life.
He freed us from the dominion of Satan, and the oppression of sin.

Our identity in Christ is a fellowship which cannot be denied.
Declaring Him as Lord sets us apart, we trust Him to lead, and to
    guide.
Praise to God our Father with thanksgiving we have victory through
    His Son,
He was the first to rise, in God's grace; we now walk together as one.

1 John 5:1

A Prayer, Praising God
with Thanksgiving

With praise and thanksgiving, Lord, I come to you in prayer,
You are faithful, You are loving, You know my every care.

With praise and thanksgiving, Lord, I trust you and believe,
Beyond my humble thinking, beyond my feeble plea
You alone see my future, God, You take great care of me.

I listen for your quiet voice which is encouragement indeed.
You decide my outcome I have all to do but heed.

With praise and thanksgiving, Lord, I come to you in prayer,
I am never disappointed for your love, your strength,
And your comfort always follows me there. Amen.

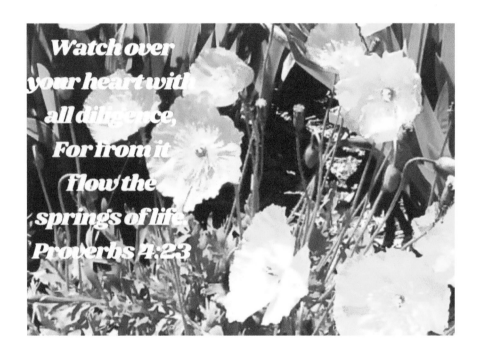

Watch over your heart with all diligence, For from it flow the springs of life. Proverbs 4:23

The Light of Christ

Don't hide your light under a bushel; it was given for a purpose,
That the world may see you have Christ in thee, and life is not
    worthless.

I, the Lord, am a beacon to the lost there is no darkness, nor a dim
    shadow,
The beam is ultrabright that all may see God's love.

Don't hide your light under a bushel; the Holy Spirit is its source,
He guides your life, have no regret, be blessed, and stay the course!

Matthew 5:16

About the Author

Alberta Betty Roveto

I was born of Italian heritage in New York City. I lived and worked most of my life in the Bronx, NY.

I Retired 2009, and since March of 2011 through e-mail Monday–Friday I send encouraging Bible Scripture to 130 contacts, my fellow-believers, family and friends. It's a commitment, I believe all need spiritual guidance when dealing with fears and doubts, stresses in business, or family matters.

In 2013 I rescued a little dog and for the past five years I am volunteering with my sweet dog Gracie, doing Pet Therapy. We make weekly visits to the hospital, and on occasion we'll visit a nursing home or make a private home visit. Through the years it's been a blessing to witness how Gracie will bring comfort and joy to people.

I started writing spiritual poems in the 1980's. It was at that time through Christian Ministry and studying God's word I learned I was worthy of God's love, that Jesus Christ's ultimate sacrifice on the cross and His resurrection gives everyone an opportunity to experience God's free gift of grace and mercy. We do not have to earn God's forgiveness or His love, just ask. I learned Satan wants to keep us under his dominion of darkness, and yes there will be challenges in our lives, but if we stay strong in faith to God regardless of circumstance, God will always be faithful to His word and His promises.

I have had no formal education in writing. I'm blessed to say my poems are a testament of God's love.

CPSIA information can be obtained
at www.ICGtesting.com
Printed in the USA
LVHW052205270121
677519LV00008B/267